HEALTHY VEGAN PERSIAN RECIPE

COPYRIGHT ©2014 BY BRYAN RYLEE.
ALL RIGHTS RESERVED. NO PART OF THIS BOOK
MAY BE USED OR REPRODUCED IN ANY MATTER
WHATSOEVER WITHOUT PERMISSION IN WRITING FROM
THE AUTHOR EXCEPT IN THE CASE OF BRIEF
QUOTATIONS
EMBODIED IN CRITICAL ARTICLES OR REVIEW.

DISCLAIMER:

THE INFORMATION PRESENTED IN THIS BOOK REPRESENTS THE VIEWS OF THE PUBLISHER AS OF THE DATE OF PUBLICATION. THE PUBLISHER RESERVES THE RIGHTS TO ALTER UPDATE THEIR OPINIONS BASED ON NEW CONDITIONS. THIS REPORT IS FOR INFORMATIONAL PURPOSES ONLY. THE AUTHOR AND THE PUBLISHER DO NOT ACCEPT ANY RESPONSIBILITIES FOR ANY LIABILITIES RESULTING FROM THE USE OF THIS INFORMATION. WHILE EVERY ATTEMPT HAS BEEN MADE TO VERIFY THE INFORMATION PROVIDED HERE, THE AUTHOR AND THE PUBLISHER CANNOT ASSUME ANY RESPONSIBILITY FOR ERRORS, INACCURACIES OR OMISSIONS. ANY SIMILARITIES WITH PEOPLE OR FACTS ARE UNINTENTIONAL.

TABLE OF CONTENTS

Introduction

The Persian Cuisine – Most Common Ingredients 10
Appetizers 13
Walnut and Cucumber Creamy Salad 13
Artichoke Heart Dip 14
Baba Ganoush 16
Green Avocado Dip on Toasted Bread 18
Beet and Walnut Dip 19
Red Bell Pepper Hummus 20
Eggplant and Tomato Fry Up 22
Potato Creamy Salad 23
Tofu and Tomato Kebabs 25
Roasted Garlic Spread 26
Salads 27
Orzo and Green Olive Salad 27
Fattoush Salad 28
Persian Carrot Salad 30
Sumac Tomato Salad 31
Persian Chickpea Salad 32
Shirazi Salad 34
Fresh Farro Salad 35
Persian Rice and Cucumber Salad 36
Soups and Stews 37
Persian Herb Soup 37
Persian Mushroom Stew 38
Persian Barley Soup – Ash-e-jow 39
Pomegranate Soup 41
Cold Cucumber Soup 42
Persian Pistachio Soup 44
Persian Herbed Bean Soup 45
Tofu Spinach Soup 46
Bean and Mushroom Stew 48

Rhubarb Stew 49
Persian Eggplant Stew 50
Persian Celery and Potato Stew 52
Lentil and Beet Soup with Flour Dumplings 53
Eggplant and Green Grape Stew 54
Main Dishes 55
Veggie Stuffed Bell Peppers 55
Persian Potato Gratin 57
Potato and Prune Casserole 59
Kateh – Persian Rice 60
Pomegranate Roasted Tofu 61
Saffron Baked Mushrooms 62
Walnut and Rice Balls 63
Persian Pilaf 65
Vegetable Curry 67
Fried Eggplant Casserole 69
Falafel Loaf 70
Persian Okra Stew 72

Persian Veggie Cabbage Rolls 73
Couscous Stuffed Tomatoes 75
Basmati Rice with Potato Crust 77
Jeweled Rice 78
Stuffed Eggplants 79
Desserts 80
Persian Melon Popsicles 80
Spiced Rice Pudding 81
Persian Chickpea Flour Cookies 82
Persian Halva 84
Spiced Carrot Halva 86
Cinnamon Date Cake 88
Wild Rice Apricot Pudding 90
Melon and Cherry Compote 91
Persian Sweet Rice 92
Ranginak – Date and Walnut Squares 93

Conclusion 94

Introduction

THE PERSIAN CUISINE INCLUDES TWO MAIN GEOGRAPHIC AREAS: PERSIA AND IRAN, AND IT IS A CUISINE THAT HAS BEEN STRONGLY INFLUENCED BY SURROUNDING AREAS, INCLUDING THE TURKISH CUISINE OR THE MEDITERRANEAN ONE, BUT ALSO INDIAN AND ASIAN. SO MUCH THAT YOU WILL FIND COMMON INGREDIENTS IN ALL OF THEM AND SOMETIMES IT IS HARD TO SAY WHICH CUISINE HAS INFLUENCED THE OTHER. BUT A FACT REMAINS – THE OLD PERSIAN ARCHIVES NAME CORIANDER, SAFFRON, CUMIN, MINT, POMEGRANATES, PISTACHIO AND EVEN OLIVE OIL AS PRODUCTS THAT WERE TRADED IN THE OLD DAYS OF THE PERSIAN EMPIRE, THEREFORE WE CAN SAY THAT THE PERSIAN CUISINE IS ANCIENT AND VARIED.

AMONGST THE STAPLE INGREDIENTS OF THE PERSIAN CUISINE YOU WILL FIND: FRESH HERBS, PLUMS, POMEGRANATES, PRUNES, APRICOTS, RAISINS, RICE, VEGETABLES, NUTS, SAFFRON, CINNAMON AND PARSLEY. THEY ARE COMBINED IN UNUSUAL WAYS SOMETIMES BUT IN THE END EVERY PERSIAN DISH IS FLAVORFUL AND RICH, DELICIOUS AND SPECIAL AND ALL YOU HAVE TO DO IS TASTE AND BE HOOKED!

ONE OF THE MOST COMMON PERSIAN INGREDIENTS, FOUND IN MANY DISHES, BOTH MEAT AND VEGAN ONES IS RICE. RICE WAS FIRST BROUGHT TO THE REGION FROM INDIA BUT IT SOON GAINED TERRAIN WITH THE LOCALS. ALTHOUGH AT FIRST IT WAS MOSTLY USED BY THE UPPER CLASS OF THE SOCIETY, IN THE LAST DECADES IT BECAME MORE ACCESSIBLE,

EVEN TO THE POOR PEOPLE WHO WENT FROM CONSUMING MOSTLY BREAD TO EATING RICE AS A BASE FOOD.

THERE ARE VARIOUS WAYS OF COOKING RICE IN THE PERSIAN CUISINE. POLO DESIGNATES THE RICE THAT IS COOKED BY SOAKING IT IN SALTED WATER FOR A FEW HOURS. THE RICE IS THEN STEAMED TO PREPARE A FLUFFY RICE THAT IT'S NOT STICKY AT ALL. THIS TYPE OF COOKED RICE IS USUALLY SERVED SIMPLE OR AS A SIDE DISH. THE SECOND WAY OF COOKING RICE INVOLVES BOILING IT IN WATER UNTIL THE LIQUID IS COMPLETELY ABSORBED. THIS METHOD IS PROBABLY THE SIMPLEST OF ALL AND IT YIELDS A SIMPLE, BASIC RICE THAT WORKS GREAT WITH SAUCES OR MOIST, JUICY DISHES. THE LAST WAY OF COOKING RICE IS CALLED *DAMY* AND IT IS VERY SIMILAR TO *KATEH* WITH THE DIFFERENCE THAT FOR *DAMY* OTHER INGREDIENTS CAN BE ADDED – NUTS, DRIED FRUITS OR VEGETABLES ARE THE MOST BASIC ADDITIONAL INGREDIENTS. OFTEN, THE RICE IS COOKED UNTIL A HARD CRUST FORMS AT THE BOTTOM – *TAH DIG*.

APART FROM RICE, BREAD IS ALSO A BIG PART OF THE PERSIAN CUISINE. THE GENERIC TERM FOR BREAD IN PERSIAN IS *NAN* WHICH YOU ARE FAMILIAR WITH SINCE *NAAN* BREAD IS AVAILABLE WORLDWIDE NOWADAYS. PERSIAN BREAD IS USUALLY ROUND OR OVAL AND FLAT AND IT IS BAKED ON A SPECIAL GRILL STOVE OR STONE. SOMETIME IS SO THIN THAT IT GOES CRISPY. BUT NO MATTER THE TYPE, BREAD IS A HUGE PART OF A MEAL IN THE PERSIAN CUISINE AND THAT SHOULDN'T BE NEGLECTED.

SINCE IT HAS MEDITERRANEAN INFLUENCES TOO, THE PERSIAN CUISINE MAKES USE OF A LOT OF FRESH FRUITS AND VEGETABLES. TRADITIONALLY, PERSIANS WOULD SERVE A BOWL OF FRESH FRUITS AT EVERY

MEAL WHILE VEGGIES ARE THE MAIN SIDE DISHES SERVED TO MOST MEALS. BUT FROM ALL THE AVAILABLE VEGETABLES, THE EGGPLANT IS THE MOST COMMON ONE. IN FACT, IT IS SO USED IN THE PERSIAN CUISINE THAT SOME PEOPLE CALL IT "THE POTATO OF PERSIA". IT IS COOKED IN WAYS THAT YOU WOULDN'T EXPECT AND IT TASTES GREAT.

BUT A PERSIAN DISH WOULDN'T BE THE SAME WITHOUT THE AROMATIC FRESH HERBS. PARSLEY, CILANTRO AND MINT ARE THE THREE MAIN HERBS USED IN ANYTHING, FROM SOUPS TO DIPS, MAIN DISHES AND SALADS. THEY ADD FRESHNESS AND MAKE DISHES LIGHTER AND HIGHLY FRAGRANT. AND SINCE WE ARE TALKING ABOUT GIVING FLAVOR TO THE FOOD, WE CAN'T NEGLECT SPICES, CAN WE?! THEY ARE VERY IMPORTANT IN MOST ORIENTAL CUISINES AND THE PERSIAN ONE IS ONE OF THEM. CINNAMON, CUMIN, SAFFRON, HOT PEPPERS AND SUMAC ARE JUST A FEW OF THE MOST USED SPICES. THEIR MAIN GOAL IS TO ADD A FRAGRANT TOUCH TO ANY DISH BUT NEVER OVERPOWER IT. ON THEIR OWN SPICES TEND TO BE INTENSE AND BOLD, BUT IN PERSIAN DISHES THEY ARE DELICATE AND SUBTLE, SUPPORTING OTHER INGREDIENTS RATHER THAN THEM BECOMING THE STARS OF THE DISH.

AN INTERESTING FACT ABOUT THE PERSIAN CUISINE IS HOW PEOPLE USED TO CHOOSE THEIR DAILY FOOD COMBINATIONS. THEY BELIEVED THAT KEEPING A BALANCE BETWEEN HOT AND COLD OR DRY AND WET IN DIET IS THE KEY TO A HEALTHY BODY AND MIND, THEREFORE THEY ALWAYS TRIED TO COMBINE A HOT FOOD WITH A COLD ONE. FAT, MEAT, WHEAT, SUGAR, DRIED FRUITS AND VEGETABLES WERE CONSIDERED HOT FOODS WHILE BEEF, RICE, DAIRY PRODUCTS AND SOME FRESH FRUITS AND VEGGIES WERE CONSIDERED COLD FOODS. WHENEVER A MENU WAS PLANNED, THIS

PRINCIPLE WAS TAKEN INTO CONSIDERATION SO THEY ALWAYS ENDED UP WITH ONE HOT FOOD AND ONE COLD FOOD ON THEIR PLATE.

AS FOR VEGANS WANTING TO EAT PERSIAN FOODS, WORRY NOT CAUSE THERE ARE PLENTY OF VEGAN RECIPES FOR EVERY TASTE OUT THERE. FROM SIMPLE RICE DISHES TO VEGETABLE DISHES, YOU WILL FIND SOMETHING TO FIT YOUR TASTE AND NEEDS IN THIS WIDE RANGE OF DISHES, ALL WITH AN AMAZING FLAVOR AND TEXTURE, ALL COLORFUL AND NUTRITIOUS.

BOTTOM LINE IS THAT THE PERSIAN CUISINE IS EXOTIC AND COLORFUL, VARIED AND FRAGRANT, FLAVORFUL AND BALANCED, IT IS A CUISINE THAT WILL TEACH ALL ABOUT SPICES, HERBS AND FRESH INGREDIENTS, A CUISINE THAT SOMEHOW MANAGES TO BALANCE INGREDIENTS THAT YOU RARELY THINK OF. ALL YOU HAVE TO DO IS KEEP AN OPEN MIND AND A BOLD PALATE AND TRY THE RECIPES FOUND IN THIS BOOK. THEY'VE ALL BEEN DESIGNED TO ACCOMMODATE THE NEEDS OF A VEGAN IN SEARCH FOR PERSIAN RECIPES SO GO AHEAD AND START COOKING. I'M SURE YOU WILL FIND A FAVORITE AMONGST THESE RECIPES!

The Persian Cuisine – Most Common Ingredients

GREEN HERBS – PARSLEY, CORIANDER, CILANTRO AND MINT ARE THE MAIN GREEN HERBS USED IN THE PERSIAN CUISINE. THEY ARE EASY TO FIND ALL YEAR AROUND IN MOST MARKETS OR SUPERMARKETS, BUT YOU CAN ALSO GROW THEM AT HOME IF YOU WANT. APART FROM THEIR INTENSE AND FRESH TASTE, GREEN HERBS ARE ALSO GREAT SOURCES OF ANTIOXIDANTS AND VITAMINS WHICH IS A GREAT ADVANTAGE IN SALADS FOR INSTANCE.

RICE – THERE ARE MANY VARIETIES OF RICE OUT THERE, BUT THE PERSIAN CUISINE USES BASMATI RICE MOSTLY. IT'S EASY TO COOK AND HAS A DELICATE TASTE THAT GOES WITH MOST FOODS. IF YOU'RE LOOKING FOR A HEALTHIER OPTION THOUGH, YOU CAN GO FOR WILD RICE WHICH HAS A MORE FLAVORFUL AROMA AS WELL.

SAFFRON – SAFFRON IS AN EXPENSIVE SPICE BECAUSE IT COMES FROM A RARE CROCUS. ONLY THE STEMS OF THE CROCUS ARE USED AND FOR THAT REASON CULTIVATING IT IS DIFFICULT. ITS TASTE IS OFTEN DESCRIBED AS HONEY WITH GRASSY NOTES. APART FROM TASTE, SAFFRON ALSO ADDS A BEAUTIFUL YELLOW-ORANGE COLOR TO ANY FOOD IS BEING USED INTO. BE CAREFUL WHEN BUYING IT THOUGH. SAFFRON IS USUALLY PACKED IN FOIL TO PROTECT FROM AIR AND LIGHT AND ONCE BOUGHT IT SHOULD BE STORED IN AIRTIGHT CONTAINERS AND DARK PLACES.

TURMERIC – ALSO KNOWN AS *CURCUMA* OR *CURCUMIN*,

TURMERIC IS A BRIGHT YELLOW POWDER MADE FROM TURMERIC RHIZOMES. IT IS AN ANCIENT SPICE THAT HAS BEEN USED IN INDIA AND SURROUNDING COUNTRIES FOR CENTURIES. IT HAS NO CALORIES AND ZERO CHOLESTEROL BUT IT IS RICH IN FIBERS, IRON, MAGNESIUM AND VITAMIN B. TURMERIC IS A GREAT SUBSTITUTE FOR SAFFRON IN TERMS OF COLOR, BUT NOT TASTE.

SUMAC – SUMAC IS LEMONY AND SALTY, A GREAT PERSIAN SPICE USED IN MANY RECIPES, FROM SALADS TO STEWS. IT IS OFTEN USED TO GIVE A CERTAIN TARTNESS TO FOODS, ALONG WITH POMEGRANATE JUICE OR SYRUP.

DRIED FRUITS – USED IN BOTH SAVORY AND SWEET DISHES, DRIED FRUITS ARE A GREAT SOURCE OF NUTRIENTS, FROM FIBERS TO VITAMINS AND MINERALS, BUT THEY ALSO PACK A LOT OF FLAVOR, USUALLY MORE FLAVOR THAN THE ACTUAL FRESH FRUITS JUST BECAUSE THEY ARE PICKED WHEN IN SEASON THEN DRIED SO THE FLAVOR INTENSIFIES AND THE AROMA IS PRESERVED. PLUS, THEY ARE EASY TO STORE IN AN AIRTIGHT CONTAINER IN YOUR CUPBOARD AND USED IN SALADS OR EVEN STEWS.

NUTS – ALMONDS, PISTACHIO AND WALNUTS ARE THREE OF THE MOST USED NUTS IN THE PERSIAN CUISINE. EITHER USED IN COOKING OR AS A SNACK, THEY ARE A GREAT SOURCE OF FIBERS AND GOOD FATS AND HAVE A RICH AROMA THAT WORKS WITH MOST FOODS.

EGGPLANTS – AS MENTIONED ABOVE, THE EGGPLANTS ARE CONSIDERED "THE POTATOES OF PERSIAN", BUT THEY HAVE FAR MORE NUTRITIOUS THAN POTATOES. IRON, CALCIUM AND FIBERS ARE JUST A FEW OF THE NUTRIENTS FOUND IN EGGPLANTS. IT'S BEEN PROVED

THAT A REGULAR INTAKE OF EGGPLANTS BOOSTS YOUR DIGESTIVE SYSTEM, BUT FURTHERMORE, EGGPLANTS HAVE LITTLE CALORIES AND LESS CARBS THAN OTHER VEGGIES.

HOWEVER, THIS IS JUST A SHORT LIST. AS LONG AS YOU USE SPICES AND HERBS YOU CAN CALL ANY RECIPE PERSIAN BECAUSE THOSE ARE THE STAPLES OF THE PERSIAN CUISINE.

AND WHEN YOU COMBINE PERSIAN WITH VEGAN, THINGS GET EVEN BETTER. VEGAN DISHES ARE DELICIOUS ON THEIR OWN, RELYING MORE ON THE PURE FLAVORS OF VEGGIES, BUT THEN YOU ADD A TOUCH OF PERSIAN AND THE DISH IMPROVES ALL OF A SUDDEN, IT GETS EVEN MORE FLAVORFUL, IT GAINS MORE AROMA AND THE VEGGIES TURN INTO REAL DELICACIES INFUSED WITH SPICES OR FRESH HERBS.

Appetizers

Walnut and Cucumber Creamy Salad

VEGAN, CREAMY AND RICH ARE THE MAIN CHARACTERISTICS OF THIS SALAD. IT'S A DELICIOUS AND NUTRITIOUS SALAD THAT CAN BE SERVED IN INDIVIDUAL PORTIONS OR TOPPED ON SOME MINI FLATBREADS.

TIME: 30 MINUTES
SERVES: 2-4

INGREDIENTS:
1 CUP RAW CASHEWS, SOAKED OVER NIGHT
4 ICE CUBES, CRUSHED
3 CUCUMBERS, DICED
1 TABLESPOON CHOPPED PARSLEY
1 TEASPOON CHOPPED MINT
1 TEASPOON CHOPPED BASIL
½ CUP WALNUTS, CHOPPED
SALT, PEPPER TO TASTE
LEMON JUICE TO TASTE

DIRECTIONS:
1. COMBINE THE CASHEWS WITH THE ICE CUBES IN A BLENDER OR FOOD PROCESSOR AND PULSE UNTIL CREAMY AND SMOOTH.
2. SPOON THE MIXTURE INTO A BOWL AND STIR IN THE REST OF THE INGREDIENTS.
3. ADD SALT AND PEPPER TO TASTE AND GARNISH WITH LEMON JUICE TO TASTE.
4. SERVE THE SALAD WITH BREAD OR EVEN VEGETABLE STICKS.

Artichoke Heart Dip

TIME: 20 MINUTES
SERVES: 4-6

INGREDIENTS:
1 JAR ARTICHOKE HEARTS, DRAINED
3 GARLIC CLOVES
1 CUP FRESH SPINACH
½ CUP SOAKED CASHEW NUTS

SALT, PEPPER TO TASTE
½ LEMON, JUICED
2 TABLESPOONS OLIVE OIL
½ TEASPOON CAPERS
½ TEASPOON DRIED MINT

DIRECTIONS:
1. MIX ALL THE INGREDIENTS IN A BLENDER OR FOOD PROCESSOR.
2. PULSE UNTIL WELL BLENDED THEN SEASON WITH SALT AND PEPPER TO TASTE.
3. SPOON THE DIP INTO A SERVING BOWL AND SERVE WITH ANYTHING FROM CHIPS TO BREAD, CROUTONS OR VEGETABLE STICKS.

Baba Ganoush

BABA GANOUSH IS ONE OF THE MOST KNOWN PERSIAN FOODS AND IT COMBINES EGGPLANTS WITH TAHINI INTO AN EARTHY, FLAVORFUL AND RICH DIP THAT TASTES GREAT WITH TOASTED BREAD.

TIME: 1 HOUR
SERVES: 4-6

INGREDIENTS:
2 LARGE EGGPLANTS
2 TABLESPOONS TAHINI PASTE
4 GARLIC CLOVES, CHOPPED
2 TABLESPOONS CHOPPED CILANTRO
JUICE FROM ½ LEMON
¼ CUP OLIVE OIL
SALT, PEPPER TO TASTE

DIRECTIONS:
1. CUT THE EGGPLANTS IN HALF LENGTHWISE AND PLACE THEM ON A BAKING TRAY.
2. BAKE THE EGGPLANTS IN THE PREHEATED OVEN AT 375F FOR 30-40 MINUTES.
3. REMOVE FROM THE OVEN WHEN THE EGGPLANTS ARE SOFT.
4. SCOOP OUT THE SOFT, CREAMY FLESH AND PLACE IT IN A FOOD PROCESSOR.
5. LET IT COOL DOWN THEN ADD THE TAHINI PASTE, GARLIC, LEMON JUICE, OLIVE OIL, SALT AND PEPPER TO TASTE AND PROCESS UNTIL SMOOTH.
6. STIR IN THE CHOPPED CILANTRO AND SERVE THE BABA GANOUSH FRESH.

Green Avocado Dip on Toasted Bread

TIME: 25 MINUTES
SERVES: 4-6

INGREDIENTS:
1 RIPE AVOCADO, PEELED
JUICE FROM ½ LEMON
½ CUP CHOPPED CILANTRO
1 GREEN ONION, CHOPPED
1 GARLIC CLOVE, MINCED
SALT, PEPPER TO TASTE
2 TABLESPOONS SOAKED CASHEW NUTS
4-6 SLICES TOASTED BREAD

DIRECTIONS:
1. COMBINE THE AVOCADO WITH THE CASHEWS AND LEMON JUICE IN A BLENDER AND PULSE UNTIL CREAMY AND SMOOTH.
2. STIR IN THE CHOPPED CILANTRO, GREEN ONION AND GARLIC THEN SEASON WITH SALT AND PEPPER.
3. SPOON THE DIP ON TOASTED BREAD AND SERVE RIGHT AWAY.

Beet and Walnut Dip

TIME: 30 MINUTES
SERVES: 2-4

INGREDIENTS:
1 LARGE COOKED BEET, GRATED
1 CUP WALNUTS, CHOPPED
1 GARLIC CLOVE, MINCED
¼ CUP VEGAN MAYONNAISE
SALT, PEPPER TO TASTE
1 TABLESPOON LEMON JUICE
CRACKERS OR TOASTED BREAD FOR SERVING

DIRECTIONS:
1. COMBINE THE BEET WITH THE WALNUTS AND GARLIC THEN STIR IN THE MAYONNAISE, LEMON JUICE, SALT AND PEPPER.
2. SPOON THE SALAD INTO A BOWL AND SERVE IT WITH CRACKERS OR TOASTED BREAD.

Red Bell Pepper Hummus

UNLIKE THE TRADITIONAL HUMMUS, THIS RECIPE IS SWEETER AND HAS A SMOKY FLAVOR THAT MAKES IT SHINE. SO STEP OUT OF YOUR COMFORT ZONE AND TRY IT. YOU WILL LOVE IT!

TIME: 20 MINUTES
SERVES: 4-6

INGREDIENTS:
2 ROASTED RED BELL PEPPERS
1 CAN CHICKPEAS, DRAINED
4 GARLIC CLOVES
¼ CUP OLIVE OIL
JUICE FROM ½ LEMON

¼ CUP TAHINI PASTE
SALT, PEPPER TO TASTE
1 PINCH CHILI POWDER
MINI FLATBREAD TO SERVE

DIRECTIONS:
1. COMBINE ALL THE INGREDIENTS IN A FOOD PROCESSOR OR BLENDER AND PULSE UNTIL WELL BLENDED AND SMOOTH.
2. SPOON THE MIXTURE IN A SERVING BOWL AND SERVE IT WITH MINI FLATBREADS.

Eggplant and Tomato Fry Up

TIME: 25 MINUTES
SERVES: 2-4

INGREDIENTS:
1 EGGPLANT, PEELED AND DICED
1 RIPE TOMATO, DICED
2 GARLIC CLOVES, CHOPPED
1 TABLESPOON TOMATO PASTE
3 TABLESPOONS OLIVE OIL
SALT, PEPPER TO TASTE

DIRECTIONS:
1. HEAT THE OLIVE OIL IN A SKILLET AND STIR IN THE GARLIC.
2. SAUTÉ FOR 30 SECONDS THEN ADD THE EGGPLANT AND SAUTÉ FOR 10 MINUTES UNTIL GOLDEN BROWN AND TENDER.
3. STIR IN THE TOMATO PASTE THEN ADD THE DICED TOMATO, AS WELL AS SALT AND PEPPER.
4. COOK THE EGGPLANT FOR 10 MORE MINUTES, STIRRING OFTEN THEN TRANSFER IT IN A SERVING BOWL.
5. IT IS BEST SERVED WITH FLATBREAD.

Potato Creamy Salad

TIME: 30 MINUTES
SERVES: 4-6

INGREDIENTS:
6 COOKED RED POTATOES, DICED
2 PICKLED CUCUMBERS, DICED
1 GREEN ONION, CHOPPED
¼ TEASPOON GARLIC POWDER
½ CUP CASHEW NUTS, SOAKED IN WATER OVERNIGHT
2 TABLESPOONS LEMON JUICE
SALT, PEPPER TO TASTE
2 TABLESPOONS CHOPPED DILL
MINI FLATBREADS TO SERVE

DIRECTIONS:

1. MIX THE CASHEWS WITH THE LEMON JUICE IN A BOWL AND PULSE UNTIL SMOOTH.
2. COMBINE THE POTATOES WITH THE CUCUMBERS, ONION, GARLIC POWDER, DILL AND CASHEW SAUCE AND MIX GENTLY.
3. SEASON WITH SALT AND PEPPER AND SERVE RIGHT AWAY.

Tofu and Tomato Kebabs

THESE KEBABS ARE A CLASSIC. YOU WILL LOVE THEIR TASTE, BUT MOST OF ALL THE EASY TECHNIQUE THAT CAN BE APPLIED TO OTHER VEGGIES OR EVEN FRUITS AS WELL.

TIME: 15 MINUTES
SERVES: 4-6

INGREDIENTS:
2 CUPS CHERRY TOMATOES
6 OZ. TOFU, CUBED
4-6 WOODEN SKEWERS

DIRECTIONS:
1. PLACE THE TOMATOES AND TOFU ON SKEWERS, ALTERNATING ONE TOMATO WITH ONE CUBE OF CHEESE.
2. SERVE THE KEBABS FRESH.

Roasted Garlic Spread

DON'T UNDERESTIMATE THIS GARLIC SPREAD. IT HAS A DELICATE GARLIC FLAVOR AND IT'S SO FLAVORFUL THAT YOU WILL WANT MORE THAN ONE SERVING.

TIME: 1 HOUR 10 MINUTES
SERVES: 4-6

INGREDIENTS:
3 LARGE GARLIC HEADS
4 TABLESPOONS OLIVE OIL
1 TEASPOON SEA SALT
1 PINCH SMOKED PAPRIKA
¼ TEASPOON DRIED MINT

DIRECTIONS:
1. CUT THE GARLIC HEAD IN HALF HORIZONTALLY THEN WRAP EACH OF THEM IN ALUMINUM FOIL.
2. PLACE THEM ALL ON A BAKING TRAY AND ROAST IN THE PREHEATED OVEN AT 330F FOR 1 HOUR.
3. REMOVE FROM THE OVEN AND CAREFULLY UNWRAP EACH HALF OF GARLIC HEAD.
4. SQUEEZE OUT THE SOFT FLESH AND PLACE IT INTO A BOWL.
5. STIR IN THE SALT, PAPRIKA AND MINT AND MIX WELL.
6. SERVE IT WARM OR CHILLED, SPREAD ON BREAD, FLATBREAD OR EVEN CHIPS.

Salads
Orzo and Green Olive Salad

TIME: 40 MINUTES
SERVES: 4-6

INGREDIENTS:
1 CUP ORZO
2 CUPS WATER OR VEGETABLE STOCK
1 CUP SPINACH
2 TABLESPOONS PINE NUTS
4 BASIL LEAVES
4 MINT LEAVES
¼ CUP OLIVE OIL
SALT, PEPPER TO TASTE
¼ LEMON, JUICED
½ CUP CHOPPED GREEN OLIVES

DIRECTIONS:
1. MIX THE ORZO WITH THE WATER OR STOCK IN A SAUCEPAN AND COOK OVER MEDIUM FLAME UNTIL THE LIQUID IS ABSORBED. REMOVE FROM HEAT AND LET IT COOL DOWN.
2. COMBINE THE SPINACH WITH THE PINE NUTS, BASIL, MINT AND OLIVE OIL IN A BLENDER AND PULSE UNTIL SMOOTH.
3. SEASON WITH SALT AND PEPPER THEN ADD THE LEMON JUICE.
4. SPOON THE PESTO OVER THE COOKED ORZO AND MIX GENTLY.
5. SERVE THE SALAD RIGHT AWAY, TOPPED WITH GREEN OLIVES.

Fattoush Salad

THIS SALAD HAS BECOME A STAPLE OF THE PERSIAN CUISINE. IT IS A MIX OF VARIOUS VEGGIES AND IT HAS SUCH A FRESH AND DELICIOUS TASTE THAT YOU WILL KEEP ASKING FOR MORE.

TIME: 30 MINUTES
SERVES: 4-6

INGREDIENTS:
1 HEAD ROMAINE LETTUCE, SHREDDED
1 SHALLOT, SLICED
2 RIPE TOMATOES, SLICED
1 CUCUMBER, SLICED
¼ CUP BLACK OLIVES, CHOPPED

1 TABLESPOON CHOPPED MINT
½ CUP CHOPPED PARSLEY
1 TABLESPOON BALSAMIC VINEGAR
2 TABLESPOONS OLIVE OIL
1 TEASPOON SUMAC
¼ TEASPOON CUMIN POWDER
SALT, PEPPER TO TASTE
2 PITA BREADS, CUBED

DIRECTIONS:
1. COMBINE ALL THE VEGGIES IN A LARGE SALAD BOWL.
2. SPRINKLE WITH SALT, PEPPER, SUMAC AND CUMIN POWDER AND MIX GENTLY, ADDING THE VINEGAR AND OLIVE OIL AS WELL.
3. GENTLY STIR IN THE CUBED FLATBREAD AND SERVE RIGHT AWAY.

Persian Carrot Salad

TIME: 20 MINUTES
SERVES: 2-4

INGREDIENTS:
2 LARGE CARROTS, FINELY GRATED
½ CUP CASHEW NUTS, SOAKED OVERNIGHT
2 TABLESPOONS LEMON JUICE
2 TABLESPOONS ORANGE JUICE
¼ TEASPOON DRIED MINT
1 PINCH CHILI POWDER
SALT, PEPPER TO TASTE
¼ CUP SLICED ALMONDS

DIRECTIONS:
1. MIX THE CASHEW NUTS WITH THE LEMON JUICE AND ORANGE JUICE IN A BLENDER AND PULSE UNTIL WELL BLENDED.
2. TRANSFER THE MIXTURE INTO A BOWL AND STIR IN THE REST OF THE INGREDIENTS.
3. SERVE THE SALAD AS FRESH AS POSSIBLE.

Sumac Tomato Salad

SALADS PLAY AN IMPORTANT PART IN THE PERSIAN CUISINE THANKS TO ITS MEDITERRANEAN INFLUENCES. AND THIS SUMAC TOMATO SALAD IS A REAL DELICACY. DON'T SKIP THE SUMAC BECAUSE IT IS THE KEY INGREDIENT AND IT YIELDS A FRAGRANT SALAD TO BE SERVED AT ANY TIME OF THE DAY.

TIME: 25 MINUTES
SERVES: 4-6

INGREDIENTS:
4 RIPE TOMATOES, SLICED
1 RED ONION, SLICED
1 CUCUMBER, SLICED
1 CUP CHOPPED PARSLEY
2 TABLESPOONS LEMON JUICE
2 TABLESPOONS OLIVE OIL
1 TEASPOON SUMAC
SALT, PEPPER TO TASTE

DIRECTIONS:
1. COMBINE ALL THE INGREDIENTS IN A BOWL.
2. MIX GENTLY AND SERVE THE SALAD AS FRESH AS POSSIBLE.

Persian Chickpea Salad

TIME: 25 MINUTES
SERVES: 4-6

INGREDIENTS:
1 CAN CHICKPEAS, DRAINED
2 TABLESPOONS OLIVE OIL
½ TEASPOON CUMIN POWDER
1 GARLIC CLOVE, CHOPPED
½ TABLESPOON GRATED GINGER
1 LIME, JUICED
1 TOMATO, DICED
½ CUP CHOPPED CILANTRO
½ CUP CHOPPED PARSLEY

SALT, PEPPER TO TASTE

DIRECTIONS:
1. COMBINE ALL THE INGREDIENTS IN A SALAD BOWL.
2. SEASON WITH SALT AND PEPPER AND SERVE THE SALAD FRESH.

Shirazi Salad

TIME: 25 MINUTES
SERVES: 2-4

INGREDIENTS:
4 RIPE TOMATOES, DICED
2 CUCUMBERS, DICED
1 RED ONION, CHOPPED
1 TABLESPOON CHOPPED MINT
½ CUP CHOPPED PARSLEY
SALT, PEPPER TO TASTE
2 TABLESPOONS OLIVE OIL
1 LIME, JUICED
¼ TEASPOON SUMAC

DIRECTIONS:
1. COMBINE ALL THE INGREDIENTS IN A BOWL AND MIX GENTLY.
2. SERVE THE SALAD AS FRESH AS POSSIBLE.

Fresh Farro Salad

TIME: 30 MINUTES
SERVES: 4-6

INGREDIENTS:
1 CUP FARRO, RINSED
3 CUPS WATER
6 RADISHES, SLICED
2 CUCUMBERS, SLICED
2 TOMATOES, SLICED
½ CUP PITTED BLACK OLIVES
1 CUP CHOPPED PARSLEY
½ CUP CHOPPED CILANTRO
¼ CUP OLIVE OIL
SALT, PEPPER TO TASTE
1 LIME, JUICED
1 TEASPOON DRIED LIME

DIRECTIONS:
1. BRING THE WATER TO A BOIL WITH A PINCH OF SALT. STIR IN THE FARO AND COOK IT UNTIL THE LIQUID IS ABSORBED. REMOVE FROM HEAT AND LET IT COOL DOWN. FLUFF IT UP WITH A FORK AND TRANSFER IT INTO A BOWL.
2. STIR IN THE REST OF THE INGREDIENTS AND MIX GENTLY.
3. SERVE THE SALAD AS FRESH AS POSSIBLE.

Persian Rice and Cucumber Salad

TIME: 50 MINUTES
SERVES: 4-6

INGREDIENTS:
1 ½ CUPS PURPLE RICE
3 CUPS WATER
1 TEASPOON CORIANDER SEEDS
4 PERSIAN CUCUMBERS, SLICED
2 GREEN ONIONS, CHOPPED
1 CUP CHOPPED PARSLEY
¼ CUP CHOPPED MINT
3 TABLESPOONS OLIVE OIL
1 TEASPOON LEMON ZEST
2 TABLESPOONS LEMON JUICE
SALT, PEPPER TO TASTE

DIRECTIONS:
1. COMBINE THE RICE WITH THE WATER AND A PINCH OF SALT AND COOK UNTIL MOST OF THE LIQUID HAS BEEN ABSORBED. REMOVE FROM HEAT AND LET IT COOL DOWN THEN TRANSFER INTO A BOWL.
2. STIR IN THE CORIANDER SEEDS, CUCUMBERS, ONIONS, PARSLEY AND MINT.
3. ADD THE LEMON ZEST, OLIVE OIL AND LEMON JUICE THEN SEASON WITH SALT AND PEPPER TO TASTE.
4. MIX GENTLY AND SERVE THE SALAD AS FRESH AS POSSIBLE.

Soups and Stews
Persian Herb Soup

TIME: 40 MINUTES
SERVES: 4-6

INGREDIENTS:
2 TABLESPOONS OLIVE OIL
1 ONION, SLICED
3 GARLIC CLOVES, CHOPPED
1 CUP CANNED CHICKPEAS, DRAINED
1 CUP CANNED WHITE BEANS, DRAINED
1 TEASPOON TURMERIC POWDER
½ TEASPOON CUMIN POWDER
1 CUP CHOPPED PARSLEY
1 CUP CHOPPED CORIANDER
¼ CUP CHOPPED MINT
2 GREEN ONIONS, CHOPPED
2 CUPS BABY SPINACH, SHREDDED
SALT, PEPPER TO TASTE
4 CUPS WATER OR VEGETABLE STOCK

DIRECTIONS:
1. HEAT THE OLIVE OIL IN A SKILLET AND STIR IN THE ONION AND GARLIC. SAUTÉ FOR 2 MINUTES THEN ADD THE CHICKPEAS, BEANS, TURMERIC AND CUMIN POWDER.
2. POUR IN THE WATER AND ADD SALT AND PEPPER TO TASTE. COOK THE SOUP FOR 15 MINUTES THEN STIR IN THE HERBS, GREEN ONIONS AND SPINACH.
3. COOK FOR 15 MORE MINUTES THEN REMOVE FROM HEAT AND SERVE THE SOUP WARM.

Persian Mushroom Stew

TIME: 1 HOUR
SERVES: 4-6

INGREDIENTS:
3 TABLESPOONS VEGETABLE OIL
1 ONION, CHOPPED
2 GARLIC CLOVES, CHOPPED
2 POUNDS MUSHROOMS, SLICED
½ TEASPOON CUMIN POWDER
SALT, PEPPER TO TASTE
2 TABLESPOONS FLOUR
1 CUP ALMOND MILK

DIRECTIONS:
1. HEAT THE OIL IN A SKILLET AND STIR IN THE ONION AND GARLIC. SAUTÉ FOR 2 MINUTES THEN ADD THE MUSHROOMS.
2. LOWER THE HEAT AND COOK THE MUSHROOMS IN THEIR OWN JUICES FOR 10-15 MINUTES.
3. MIX WELL THE FLOUR WITH THE MILK AND POUR IT IN THE PAN OVER THE MUSHROOMS.
4. COOK UNTIL IT BEGINS TO THICKEN THEN ADJUST THE TASTE WITH SALT, PEPPER AND CUMIN POWDER.
5. REMOVE FROM HEAT AND SERVE IT WARM.

Persian Barley Soup – Ash-e-jow

BARLEY IS A GREAT ALTERNATIVE TO RICE OR OTHER KIND OF GRAIN. IT HAS A HIGH NUTRITIONAL CONTENT AND A NUTTY, EARTHY FLAVOR THAT WORKS GREAT IN SOUPS, AS WELL AS STEWS OR SALADS.

TIME: 40 MINUTES
SERVES: 4-6

INGREDIENTS:
2 TABLESPOONS OLIVE OIL
1 ONION, CHOPPED
1 GARLIC CLOVE, CHOPPED
1 CUP UNCOOKED BARLEY, RINSED
4 CUPS VEGETABLE STOCK
½ TEASPOON TURMERIC POWDER
½ TEASPOON CUMIN POWDER
1 LIME, JUICED
2 TOMATOES, DICED
1 CARROT, DICED
SALT, PEPPER TO TASTE
2 TABLESPOONS CHOPPED PARSLEY

DIRECTIONS:
1. HEAT THE OLIVE OIL IN A SOUP POT AND STIR IN THE ONION AND GARLIC. SAUTÉ FOR 2 MINUTES THEN ADD THE BARLEY, TURMERIC AND CUMIN.
2. SAUTÉ FOR 2 MORE MINUTES THEN STIR IN THE TOMATOES AND CARROT.
3. POUR IN THE STOCK THEN SEASON WITH SALT AND PEPPER AND COOK FOR 20-30 MINUTES ON LOW HEAT.
4. WHEN DONE, REMOVE FROM HEAT AND

STIR IN THE CHOPPED PARSLEY.
5. SERVE THE SOUP WARM AND FRESH.

Pomegranate Soup

ALTHOUGH SLIGHTLY UNUSUAL, THIS SOUP IS A TANGY DELICACY. IF YOU LIKE BOLD FOODS, THIS IS THE ONE FOR YOU.

TIME: 1 HOUR
SERVES: 4-6

INGREDIENTS:
2 CUPS VEGETABLE STOCK
4 CUPS WATER
½ TEASPOON TURMERIC POWDER
1 CUP SHORT GRAIN RICE, RINSED
2 BEETS, GRATED
1 CUP POMEGRANATE JUICE
½ CUP CHOPPED PARSLEY
½ CUP CHOPPED CILANTRO
1 TEASPOON DRIED MINT
SALT, PEPPER TO TASTE

DIRECTIONS:
1. COMBINE THE WATER WITH THE STOCK, RICE, TURMERIC AND BEETS IN A SOUP POT.
2. ADD SALT AND PEPPER TO TASTE AND COOK FOR 20-30 MINUTES.
3. STIR IN THE REST OF THE INGREDIENTS AND COOK 10 MORE MINUTES.
4. REMOVE FROM HEAT AND LET IT COOL DOWN BEFORE SERVING.

Cold Cucumber Soup

TIME: 20 MINUTES
SERVES: 2-4

INGREDIENTS:
2 LARGE CUCUMBERS
1 CUP CASHEW NUTS, SOAKED OVERNIGHT
½ CUP CRUSHED ICE
½ CUP WATER
2 GARLIC CLOVES
½ LEMON, JUICED
2 TABLESPOONS OLIVE OIL FOR SERVING

1 TABLESPOON CHOPPED DILL
SALT, PEPPER TO TASTE

DIRECTIONS:
1. COMBINE THE CUCUMBERS WITH THE CASHEWS, ICE, WATER, GARLIC AND LEMON JUICE IN A BLENDER. ADD THE DILL AND PULSE AGAIN.
2. ADD SALT AND PEPPER TO TASTE AND PULSE UNTIL WELL BLENDED AND SMOOTH.
3. TOP WITH A DRIZZLE OF OLIVE OIL BEFORE SERVING.

Persian Pistachio Soup

TIME: 1 HOUR
SERVES: 4-6

INGREDIENTS:
1 CUP SHELLED PISTACHIO
2 TABLESPOONS OLIVE OIL
1 SHALLOT, CHOPPED
1 LEEK, CHOPPED
2 GARLIC CLOVES, CHOPPED
2 TABLESPOONS ALL PURPOSE FLOUR
6 CUPS VEGETABLE STOCK
2 TABLESPOONS LEMON JUICE
SALT, PEPPER TO TASTE
2 TABLESPOONS CHOPPED CILANTRO

DIRECTIONS:
1. GROUND THE PISTACHIO IN A FOOD PROCESSOR AND SET ASIDE.
2. HEAT THE OIL IN A SOUP POT AND STIR IN THE SHALLOT, GARLIC AND LEEK. SAUTÉ FOR 5 MINUTES THEN STIR IN THE FLOUR.
3. POUR IN THE STOCK THEN STIR IN THE PISTACHIO AND LEMON JUICE.
4. ADD SALT AND PEPPER TO TASTE AND COOK THE SOUP FOR 40 MINUTES ON LOW HEAT.
5. PUREE THE SOUP WITH AN IMMERSION BLENDER.
6. SERVE THE SOUP FRESH, TOPPED WITH CHOPPED CILANTRO.

Persian Herbed Bean Soup

TIME: 1 HOUR
SERVES: 4-6

INGREDIENTS:
2 TABLESPOONS OLIVE OIL
1 LARGE ONION, CHOPPED
2 GARLIC CLOVES, CHOPPED
3 CUPS CANNED KIDNEY BEANS, DRAINED
1 TEASPOON TURMERIC
4 CUPS WATER
1 CUP VEGETABLE STOCK
1 CUP CHOPPED PARSLEY
1 CUP CHOPPED CILANTRO
1 CUP CHOPPED CHIVES
SALT, PEPPER TO TASTE
1 LIME, JUICED

DIRECTIONS:
1. HEAT THE OLIVE OIL IN A SOUP POT AND STIR IN THE ONION AND GARLIC. SAUTÉ FOR 2 MINUTES THEN STIR IN THE BEANS, TURMERIC, WATER AND STOCK.
2. COOK THE BEANS FOR 15 MINUTES THEN STIR IN THE HERBS.
3. SEASON WITH SALT AND PEPPER TO TASTE AND COOK 15-20 MORE MINUTES.
4. GARNISH THE SOUP WITH LIME JUICE AND SERVE IT WARM AND FRESH.

Tofu Spinach Soup

TIME: 45 MINUTES
SERVES: 4-6

INGREDIENTS:
10 OZ FIRM TOFU, CUBED
3 TABLESPOONS VEGETABLE OIL
1 TEASPOON TURMERIC POWDER
1 LARGE ONION, FINELY CHOPPED
4 GARLIC CLOVES, CHOPPED
2 CUPS CANNED KIDNEY BEANS, DRAINED
4 CUPS VEGETABLE STOCK
4 CUPS FRESH SPINACH, SHREDDED
1 CUP CHOPPED PARSLEY
½ CUP CHOPPED CORIANDER
SALT, PEPPER TO TASTE
1 LIME, JUICED

DIRECTIONS:
1. HEAT THE OIL IN A SOUP POT AND STIR IN THE TOFU. SAUTÉ FOR 5 MINUTES UNTIL GOLDEN BROWN ON ALL SIDES THEN STIR IN THE TURMERIC POWDER, ONION AND GARLIC.
2. SAUTÉ FOR 5 MORE MINUTES, STIRRING OFTEN THEN ADD THE BEANS AND STOCK.
3. SEASON WITH SALT AND PEPPER AND COOK THE SOUP FOR 25 MINUTES.
4. STIR IN THE PARSLEY, CORIANDER AND SPINACH AND COOK FOR 15 MORE MINUTES.
5. GARNISH THE SOUP WITH LIME JUICE THEN REMOVE IT FROM HEAT AND LET IT COOL DOWN SLIGHTLY.
6. SERVE THE SOUP FRESH.

Bean and Mushroom Stew

TIME: 1 HOUR
SERVES: 4-6

INGREDIENTS:
2 TABLESPOONS VEGETABLE OIL
1 ONION, SLICED
4 GARLIC CLOVES, CHOPPED
2 POUNDS MUSHROOMS, SLICED
2 CUPS CANNED BLACK BEANS, DRAINED
1 CUP TOMATO PUREE
1 CUP VEGETABLE STOCK
1 TEASPOON TURMERIC POWDER
¼ TEASPOON CAYENNE PEPPER
2 SWEET POTATOES, PEELED AND CUBED
SALT, PEPPER TO TASTE
¼ CUP CHOPPED CILANTRO

DIRECTIONS:
1. HEAT THE OIL IN A HEAVY SAUCEPAN AND STIR IN THE ONION AND GARLIC. SAUTÉ FOR 2 MINUTES THEN ADD THE MUSHROOMS, BEANS, TURMERIC, CAYENNE PEPPER AND SWEET POTATOES.
2. SAUTÉ FOR 5 MORE MINUTES THEN POUR IN THE TOMATO PUREE AND STOCK.
3. SEASON WITH SALT AND PEPPER TO TASTE AND COOK THE SOUP OVER MEDIUM FLAME FOR 30-40 MINUTES.
4. WHEN DONE, REMOVE FROM HEAT AND STIR IN THE CILANTRO.
5. SERVE THE STEW WARM AND FRESH.

Rhubarb Stew

YES, YOU READ THAT RIGHT! A SAVORY STEW WITH RHUBARB! YOU WILL BE SURPRISED TO DISCOVER A TANGY, DELICATE STEW THAT OFFERS A GREAT EXPERIENCE FOR A BOLD PALATE.

TIME: 1 HOUR
SERVES: 2-4

INGREDIENTS:
1 ONION, FINELY CHOPPED
1 LARGE CARROT, SLICED
1 CUP WATER
3 CUPS CHOPPED PARSLEY
1 TEASPOON TURMERIC POWDER
½ TEASPOON SAFFRON STRANDS
1 POUND FRESH RHUBARB, CUT INTO 1-INCH PIECES
SALT, PEPPER TO TASTE
COOKED RICE FOR SERVING

DIRECTIONS:
1. COMBINE THE ONION, WATER AND CARROT IN A SAUCEPAN. COOK FOR 10 MINUTES THEN ADD THE TURMERIC, SAFFRON AND RHUBARB.
2. LOWER THE HEAT AND COOK THE STEW FOR 15-20 MINUTES.
3. ADD SALT AND PEPPER TO TASTE THEN STIR IN THE PARSLEY.

COOK 10 MORE MINUTES THEN REMOVE FROM HEAT AND SERVE THE STEW WARM WITH COOKED RICE.

Persian Eggplant Stew

EGGPLANTS ARE HIGHLY USED IN THE PERSIAN CUISINE AND THE TRUTH IS THAT ALL THE DISHES USING THEM ARE FLAVORFUL AND DELICIOUS. THESE SUMMER VEGETABLES CAN BECOME REAL DELICACIES IF COOKED FOLLOWING A PERSIAN RECIPE.

TIME: 1 HOUR
SERVES: 4-6
INGREDIENTS:
2 ONIONS, CHOPPED
4 TABLESPOONS OLIVE OIL

2 GARLIC CLOVES, CHOPPED
2 LARGE EGGPLANTS, PEELED AND CUBED
2 RIPE TOMATOES, DICED
½ TEASPOON CUMIN POWDER
1 TEASPOON TURMERIC
1 CUP TOMATO SAUCE
1 CUP VEGETABLE STOCK
SALT, PEPPER TO TASTE
DIRECTIONS:
1. HEAT THE OIL IN A SKILLET AND STIR IN THE ONIONS AND GARLIC. SAUTÉ FOR 5-7 MINUTES.
2. STIR IN THE EGGPLANTS AND TOMATOES, AS WELL AS CUMIN POWDER AND TURMERIC AND SAUTÉ FOR 5 MORE MINUTES.
3. ADD THE STOCK AND TOMATO SAUCE THEN SEASON WITH SALT AND PEPPER TO TASTE. LOWER THE HEAT AND COOK THE STEW FOR 30 MINUTES.
4. SERVE THE STEW WARM AND FRESH.

Persian Celery and Potato Stew

TIME: 1 HOUR
SERVES: 4-6

INGREDIENTS:
4 TABLESPOONS VEGETABLE OIL
3 CELERY STALKS, CHOPPED
1 ONION, CHOPPED
2 GARLIC CLOVES, CHOPPED
1 TEASPOON DRIED MINT
½ TEASPOON TURMERIC
2 CUPS TOMATO PUREE
1 CUP VEGETABLE STOCK
1 BAY LEAF
1 ½ POUNDS POTATOES, PEELED AND CUBED
SALT, PEPPER TO TASTE
1 LIME, JUICED

DIRECTIONS:
1. HEAT THE OIL IN A SOUP POT AND STIR IN THE CELERY, POTATOES, ONION AND GARLIC.
2. SAUTÉ FOR 5-10 MINUTES, STIRRING OFTEN THEN ADD THE DRIED MINT AND TURMERIC.
3. POUR IN THE TOMATO PUREE AND STOCK THEN ADD THE BAY LEAF, SALT AND PEPPER TO TASTE.
4. COOK THE STEW FOR 30-40 MINUTES UNTIL THE POTATOES ARE TENDER.
5. ADD THE LIME JUICE AND SERVE THE STEW WARM.

Lentil and Beet Soup with Flour Dumplings

TIME: 1 HOUR
SERVES: 4-6

INGREDIENTS:
SOUP:
1 CUP LENTILS, RINSED
2 MEDIUM SIZE BEETROOTS, GRATED
1 ONION, CHOPPED
5 CUPS VEGETABLE STOCK
½ TEASPOON DRIED MINT
½ CUP CHOPPED DILL
½ CUP CHOPPED PARSLEY
½ TEASPOON TURMERIC
SALT, PEPPER TO TASTE
1 LIME, JUICED
DUMPLINGS:
½ CUP ALL PURPOSE FLOUR
¼ CUP WARM WATER

DIRECTIONS:
1. TO MAKE THE SOUP, COMBINE ALL THE INGREDIENTS IN A SOUP BOWL AND COOK ON LOW HEAT UNTIL THE LENTILS ARE COOKED THROUGH, AROUND 30 MINUTES.
2. SEASON THE SOUP WITH SALT AND PEPPER.
3. TO MAKE THE DUMPLINGS, COMBINE THE FLOUR WITH THE WATER.
4. DROP PIECES OF DOUGH IN THE BOILING SOUP AND COOK JUST 5-7 MORE MINUTES.
REMOVE FROM HEAT AND LET IT COOL DOWN SLIGHTLY BEFORE SERVING.

Eggplant and Green Grape Stew

THIS STEW WILL SURPRISE YOU FOR SURE. IT IS RICH AND FLAVORFUL, BUT THE GRAPES CUT DOWN THROUGH THAT RICHNESS WITH THEIR DELICATE TANGINESS. OVERALL, IT IS A BALANCED AND DELICIOUS STEW THAT WILL MAKE YOU STEP OUT OF YOUR COMFORT ZONE.

TIME: 1 HOUR
SERVES: 4-6

INGREDIENTS:
3 EGGPLANTS, PEELED AND DICED
2 GARLIC CLOVES, CHOPPED
1 SHALLOT, SLICED
4 TABLESPOONS OLIVE OIL
1 TEASPOON DRIED MINT
½ TEASPOON SUMAC
1 CUP SEEDLESS GRAPES
SALT, PEPPER TO TASTE
4 RIPE TOMATOES, SLICED

DIRECTIONS:
1. HEAT THE OIL IN A SKILLET AND STIR IN THE GARLIC AND SHALLOT. SAUTÉ FOR 2 MINUTES THEN ADD THE MIN, SUMAC AND EGGPLANT.
2. SAUTÉ FOR 5-10 MINUTES THEN ADD THE GRAPES AND TOMATOES.
3. SEASON WITH SALT AND PEPPER THEN LOWER THE HEAT AND COOK THE STEW IN ITS OWN JUICE FOR 30-40 MINUTES. IF NEEDED, ADD A BIT OF WATER.
4. WHEN DONE, REMOVE FROM HEAT AND LET IT COOL DOWN COMPLETELY BEFORE SERVING.

Main Dishes
Veggie Stuffed Bell Peppers

THIS VERSATILE RECIPE IS A GREAT CHOICE FOR LUNCH OR DINNER. THE PEPPERS CAN BE MADE AHEAD OF TIME, COOKED THEN FROZEN AND JUST REHEATED WHEN YOU WANT SOME PERSIAN FLAVORS FLOODING YOUR SENSES.

TIME: 1 ½ HOURS
SERVES: 6

INGREDIENTS:

6 GREEN OR RED BELL PEPPERS
4 CARROTS, GRATED
2 ONIONS, CHOPPED
4 TABLESPOONS OLIVE OIL
1 CUP RICE, RINSED
½ CUP TOMATO PASTE
1 CUP CHOPPED PARSLEY
1 CUP CHOPPED CILANTRO
1 TEASPOON DRIED MINT
1 TEASPOON DRIED THYME
¼ TEASPOON CUMIN POWDER
SALT, PEPPER TO TASTE
2 CUPS VEGETABLE STOCK
1 CUP TOMATO PUREE
1 BAY LEAF

DIRECTIONS:
1. CUT THE TOP OF EACH BELL PEPPER AND REMOVE THE CORE. SET ASIDE.
2. HEAT THE OIL IN A SKILLET AND STIR IN THE CARROTS AND ONIONS. SAUTÉ FOR 10 MINUTES THEN ADD THE RICE AND TOMATO PASTE.
3. MIX WELL AND COOK 5 MORE MINUTE THEN REMOVE FROM HEAT AND STIR IN THE PARSLEY, CILANTRO, MINT, THYME AND CUMIN POWDER.
4. SEASON WITH SALT AND PEPPER THEN FILL EACH PEPPER WITH THIS MIXTURE.
5. PLACE THEM ALL IN A SOUP POT AND POUR IN THE STOCK AND TOMATO PUREE.
6. ADD THE BAY LEAF, A PINCH OF SALT AND COOK ON LOW HEAT FOR 1 HOUR.
7. SERVE THE PEPPERS WARM.

Persian Potato Gratin

TIME: 1 ½ HOURS
SERVES: 6-8

INGREDIENTS:
2 POUND RED POTATOES, PEELED AND FINELY SLICED
10 OZ. CREAMY TOFU
1 CUP ALMOND MILK
2 TABLESPOONS COCONUT OIL
1 TEASPOON DRIED MINT
½ TEASPOON DRIED THYME
½ TEASPOON DRIED OREGANO
1 TEASPOON GARLIC POWDER
SALT, PEPPER TO TASTE

DIRECTIONS:
1. COMBINE THE TOFU WITH THE MILK, COCONUT OIL, HERBS AND GARLIC POWDER IN A BLENDER AND PULSE UNTIL SMOOTH.
2. ADD SALT AND PEPPER TO TASTE IF NEEDED.
3. IN A SMALL DEEP DISH BAKING PAN, LAYER THE THIN POTATO SLICES WITH THE TOFU MIXTURE, FINISHING WITH A LAYER OF TOFU.
4. BAKE THE GRATIN IN THE PREHEATED OVEN AT 350F FOR 40-50 MINUTES UNTIL TENDER AND FRAGRANT.
5. SERVE THE POTATOES WARM.

Potato and Prune Casserole

THIS IS DEFINITELY NOT YOUR USUAL CASSEROLE, BUT DON'T AVOID IT! DRIED PRUNES ARE A GREAT SOURCE OF NUTRIENTS AND FLAVOR, ESPECIALLY IF YOU CAN FIND THE SMOKED ONES.

TIME: 1 HOUR
SERVES: 4-6

INGREDIENTS:
2 POUNDS RED POTATOES, PEELED AND CUBED
2 CUPS PITTED PRUNES, COARSELY CHOPPED
1 ONION, CHOPPED
2 TABLESPOONS OLIVE OIL
2 GARLIC CLOVES, CHOPPED
SALT, PEPPER TO TASTE
2 CUPS TOMATO SAUCE
½ TEASPOON CUMIN POWDER
1 PINCH CHILI FLAKES
½ TEASPOON SAFFRON

DIRECTIONS:
1. HEAT THE OLIVE OIL IN A FRYING PAN AND STIR IN THE ONION AND GARLIC. SAUTÉ FOR 2 MINUTES THEN ADD THE POTATOES AND PRUNES.
2. SAUTÉ FOR 10 MINUTES, STIRRING IN THE CUMIN POWDER, CHILI AND SAFFRON.
3. TRANSFER THE MIXTURE IN A DEEP DISH BAKING PAN AND POUR THE TOMATO SAUCE OVER THE POTATOES.
4. COOK IN THE PREHEATED OVEN AT 350F FOR 40-50 MINUTES.
5. REMOVE FROM HEAT WHEN DONE AND SERVE WARM.

Kateh – Persian Rice

TIME: 10 MINUTES
SERVES: 4-6

INGREDIENTS:
4 CUPS COOKED BASMATI RICE
2 TABLESPOONS VEGETABLE OIL
1 TEASPOON DRIED MINT
SALT, PEPPER TO TASTE

DIRECTIONS:
1. HEAT THE OIL IN A SKILLET. STIR IN THE RICE AND FRY IT A FEW MINUTES, STIRRING OFTEN.
2. ADD THE MINT AND SEASON WITH SALT AND PEPPER.
3. SERVE THE RICE WARM.

Pomegranate Roasted Tofu

INFUSED WITH POMEGRANATE JUICE TOFU TURNS INTO A DELICATE AND DELICIOUS ROAST THAT CAN BE SERVED WITH ANY SIDE DISH YOU LIKE.

TIME: 45 MINUTES
SERVES: 4

INGREDIENTS:
4 THICK SLICES TOFU
1 CUP POMEGRANATE JUICE
1 TABLESPOON SOY SAUCE
1 SHALLOT, CHOPPED
4 TABLESPOONS OLIVE OIL
1 PINCH BLACK PEPPER

DIRECTIONS:
1. COMBINE THE POMEGRANATE JUICE WITH THE SOY SAUCE AND SHALLOT IN A BOWL.
2. ADD THE TOFU SLICES AND LET THEM MARINATE FOR 30 MINUTES AT LEAST.
3. DRAIN THEM AND PLACE THEM ON A BAKING TRAY.
4. SPRINKLE WITH BLACK PEPPER AND DRIZZLE WITH OIL.
5. ROAST THE TOFU IN THE PREHEATED OVEN AT 400F FOR 15-20 MINUTES.
6. SERVE IT WARM WITH YOUR FAVORITE SIDE DISH.

Saffron Baked Mushrooms

TIME: 40 MINUTES
SERVES: 6

INGREDIENTS:
6 PORTOBELLO MUSHROOMS
1 ONION, FINELY CHOPPED
2 TABLESPOONS OLIVE OIL
2 GARLIC CLOVES, CHOPPED
1 CUP GROUND ALMONDS
1 TEASPOON DRIED MINT
SALT, PEPPER TO TASTE
½ TEASPOON SAFFRON

DIRECTIONS:
1. HEAT THE OIL IN A SKILLET AND STIR IN THE ONION AND GARLIC. SAUTÉ FOR 2 MINUTES THEN REMOVE FROM HEAT AND ADD THE GROUND ALMONDS, SAFFRON AND MINT.
2. SEASON WITH SALT AND PEPPER THEN SPOON THE MIXTURE INTO EACH MUSHROOM CAP.
3. PLACE THEM ALL ON A BAKING TRAY AND BAKE IN THE PREHEATED OVEN AT 350F FOR 30 MINUTES.
4. LET THEM COOL DOWN A FEW MINUTES BEFORE SERVING.

Walnut and Rice Balls

IT'S NOT UNUSUAL FOR THE PERSIAN CUISINE TO USE WALNUTS OR OTHER KIND OF NUTS. BUT EVEN MORE UNUSUAL IS THAT THESE NUTS ARE BEING USED IN SAVORY FOODS, SUCH AS THESE RICE BALLS.

TIME: 1 HOUR
SERVES: 8

INGREDIENTS:
4 CUPS COOKED SHORT GRAIN RICE
1 CUP GROUND WALNUTS
¼ CUP CHICKPEA FLOUR
¼ CUP CHOPPED PARSLEY
1 TABLESPOON CHOPPED TARRAGON
1 TEASPOON DRIED MINT
1 TEASPOON TURMERIC POWDER
½ TEASPOON CUMIN POWDER
SALT, PEPPER TO TASTE
WATER TO COOK THEM

DIRECTIONS:
1. POUR A FEW CUPS OF WATER IN A LARGE POT AND BRING TO A BOIL WITH A PINCH OF SALT. LET IT COME TO A BOIL WHILE YOU MAKE THE RICE BALLS.
2. COMBINE THE RICE WITH THE REST OF THE INGREDIENTS IN A LARGE BOWL. SEASON WITH SALT AND PEPPER THEN WET YOUR HANDS AND FORM MEDIUM SIZE BALLS.
3. DROP THEM ALL IN THE HOT, BOILING WATER TRYING NOT TO CROWD THEM. AT FIRST THEY WILL SINK BUT AS THEY COOK THEY WILL COME TO THE SURFACE. AFTER 3-4 MINUTES THEY ARE DONE. CAREFULLY DRAIN THEM AND

SERVE THEM AS MAIN DISH OR SIDE DISH.

Persian Pilaf

PILAF IS A RICE DISH BUT IT'S VERSATILE AND RICH, PERFECT FOR LUNCH OR DINNER AND SUITED FOR THE ENTIRE FAMILY.

TIME: 1 HOUR
SERVES: 4-6

INGREDIENTS:
2 TABLESPOONS OLIVE OIL
1 SHALLOT CHOPPED
1 CARROT, DICED
½ CELERY STALK, DICED
½ CUP RAISINS

1 TEASPOON DRIED MINT
1 TEASPOON GRATED GINGER
1 TEASPOON TURMERIC
1 CUP SHORT GRAIN RICE, RINSED
3 CUPS VEGETABLE STOCK

DIRECTIONS:
1. HEAT THE OIL IN A HEAVY SAUCEPAN AND STIR IN THE SHALLOT, CARROT AND CELERY. SAUTÉ FOR 2 MINUTES THEN STIR IN THE RAISINS, MINT, GINGER, TURMERIC AND RICE.
2. SAUTÉ FOR 2 MORE MINUTES THEN ADD THE STOCK.
3. LOWER THE HEAT, COVER WITH A LID AND COOK THE PILAF FOR 30 MINUTES UNTIL MOST OF THE LIQUID HAS BEEN ABSORBED.
4. REMOVE FROM HEAT AND SERVE THE PILAF WARM.

Vegetable Curry

THE GREAT THING ABOUT THIS RECIPE IS THAT YOU CAN USE ANY VEGETABLES YOU WANT AND IT WILL STILL TASTE GREAT AND BE RICH AND FLAVORFUL.

TIME: 1 HOUR
SERVES: 4-6

INGREDIENTS:
1 ONION, CHOPPED
2 GARLIC CLOVES, CHOPPED
2 TABLESPOONS VEGETABLE OIL
1 LARGE CARROT, SLICED
1 POUND RED POTATOES, PEELED AND CUBED
1 POUND SWEET POTATOES, PEELED AND CUBED
2 TABLESPOONS CURRY PASTE
1 TEASPOON TURMERIC POWDER
1 CUP VEGETABLE STOCK
1 CUP COCONUT MILK
SALT, PEPPER TO TASTE
1 BAY LEAF

DIRECTIONS:
1. HEAT THE OIL IN A HEAVY SAUCEPAN AND STIR IN THE ONION AND GARLIC. SAUTÉ FOR 2 MINUTES UNTIL SOFT AND TRANSLUCENT THEN STIR IN THE CARROT AND POTATOES.
2. SAUTÉ FOR 5 MINUTES, STIRRING OFTEN, THEN ADD THE CURRY PASTE, TURMERIC POWDER, STOCK AND COCONUT MILK.
3. ADD SALT AND PEPPER TO TASTE, AS WELL AS ONE BAY LEAF AND COOK THE CURRY ON LOW TO MEDIUM HEAT FOR 30-40 MINUTES UNTIL THE VEGGIES ARE TENDER.
4. REMOVE FROM HEAT AND SERVE THE

CURRY WARM.

Fried Eggplant Casserole

TIME: 1 HOUR
SERVES: 4-6

INGREDIENTS:
2 LARGE EGGPLANTS, PEELED AND CUBED
¼ CUP VEGETABLE OIL
1 CAN DICED TOMATOES
½ CUP TOMATO JUICE
1 TEASPOON DRIED MINT
1 TEASPOON DRIED BASIL
½ TEASPOON GROUND GINGER
SALT, PEPPER TO TASTE

DIRECTIONS:
1. HEAT THE OIL IN A SKILLET AND STIR IN THE EGGPLANT.
2. FRY FOR 10 MINUTES, STIRRING OFTEN THEN ADD THE REST OF THE INGREDIENTS.
3. SEASON WITH SALT AND PEPPER AND TRANSFER THE EGGPLANT IN A DEEP DISH BAKING PAN.
4. BAKE THE EGGPLANT IN THE PREHEATED OVEN AT 350F FOR 20-30 MINUTES.
5. SERVE THE CASSEROLE WARM.

Falafel Loaf

FALAFEL HAS A BALL SHAPE USUALLY BUT IT CAN TIME CONSUMING SHAPED LIKE THAT. THIS VERSION IS MUCH EASIER BECAUSE THE MIXTURE IS BAKED IN A LOAF PAN AND THE RESULT IS A FLAVORFUL AND DELICIOUS LOAF THAT CAN BE EVEN FROZEN FOR LATER SERVING IF YOU WANT.

TIME: 1 ¼ HOURS
SERVES: 6-8

INGREDIENTS:
2 CANS CHICKPEAS, DRAINED
1 CUP TOMATO SAUCE
½ CUP GROUND FLAX SEEDS
½ CUP COLD WATER
1 POUND BABY CARROTS, DICED
1 ONION, FINELY CHOPPED
4 GARLIC CLOVES, CHOPPED
1 CUP CHOPPED PARSLEY
SALT, PEPPER TO TASTE
¼ CUP OLIVE OIL

DIRECTIONS:
1. PLACE THE CHICKPEAS IN A FOOD PROCESSOR AND PULSE UNTIL GROUND.
2. IN A BOWL, COMBINE THE GROUND FLAX SEEDS WITH THE WATER AND LET THEM SOAK 10 MINUTES.
3. STIR IN THE CHICKPEAS, TOMATO SAUCE, CARROTS, ONION, GARLIC AND PARSLEY.
4. ADD SALT AND PEPPER TO TASTE AND MIX WELL THEN STIR IN THE OLIVE OIL AND SPOON THE MIXTURE INTO A LOAF PAN LINED WITH

PARCHMENT PAPER.
5. BAKE THE FALAFEL LOAF IN THE PREHEATED OVEN AT 350F FOR 40 MINUTES.
6. REMOVE FROM THE OVEN AND LET IT COOL DOWN BEFORE SERVING.

Persian Okra Stew

TIME: 1 HOUR
SERVES: 6-8

INGREDIENTS:
3 TABLESPOONS VEGETABLE OIL
1 ONION, CHOPPED
2 GARLIC CLOVES, CHOPPED
1 CARROT, DICED
2 POUND OKRA, TRIMMED AND HALVED
1 CUP DICED TOMATOES
1 CUP TOMATO PUREE
1 TEASPOON DRIED MINT
½ TEASPOON DRIED THYME
SALT, PEPPER TO TASTE
2 TABLESPOONS CHOPPED PARSLEY
2 TABLESPOONS CHOPPED CILANTRO

DIRECTIONS:
1. HEAT THE OIL IN A SAUCEPAN AND STIR IN THE ONION, GARLIC AND CARROT.
2. SAUTÉ FOR 2-3 MINUTES THEN ADD THE OKRA, TOMATOES AND TOMATO PUREE.
3. STIR IN THE MINT AND THYME THEN SEASON WITH SALT AND PEPPER TO TASTE.
4. COOK THE STEW FOR 30-40 MINUTES ON LOW HEAT.
5. WHEN DONE, REMOVE THE STEW FROM HEAT AND STIR IN THE CHOPPED HERBS.
6. SERVE IT WARM AND FRESH.

Persian Veggie Cabbage Rolls

CABBAGE ROLLS CAN BE FOUND IN MANY PARTS OF THE GLOBE, BUT NONE OF THEM TASTES AS FRESH AND BOLD AS THESE ONES.

TIME: 1 ½ HOURS
SERVES: 8-10

INGREDIENTS:
1 LARGE CABBAGE
4 TABLESPOONS VEGETABLE OIL
2 ONIONS, FINELY CHOPPED
1 LARGE CARROT, FINELY CHOPPED
2 GARLIC CLOVES, CHOPPED
1 CELERY STALK, CHOPPED
1 CUP SHORT GRAIN RICE, RINSED
1 CUP CANNED CHICKPEAS, DRAINED
1 CUP CHOPPED PARSLEY
1 CUP CHOPPED CILANTRO
¼ CUP CHOPPED MINT
2 GREEN ONIONS, CHOPPED
SALT, PEPPER TO TASTE
1 LEMON, JUICED
4 CUPS WATER
1 TEASPOON DRIED THYME
1 BAY LEAF

DIRECTIONS:
1. HEAT THE OIL IN A SKILLET AND STIR IN THE ONIONS, CARROT, GARLIC AND CELERY.
2. SAUTÉ FOR 10 MINUTES, STIRRING OFTEN, THEN ADD THE RICE AND COOK 5 MORE MINUTES.
3. REMOVE FROM HEAT AND STIR IN THE CHOPPED HERBS, CHICKPEAS AND GREEN

ONIONS.
4. ADD SALT AND PEPPER TO TASTE AND LET THE MIXTURE COOL DOWN.
5. CAREFULLY PEEL THE CABBAGE, LEAF BY LEAF AND SET ASIDE.
6. POUR A FEW CUPS OF WATER IN A LARGE POT AND BRING TO A BOIL. THROW IN THE CABBAGE LEAVES AND COOK THEM JUST A FEW MINUTES TO SOFTEN THEM.
7. DRAIN AND LET THEM COOL DOWN.
8. TO FINISH THE ROLLS, TAKE ONE LEAF OF CABBAGE AND PLACE A FEW SPOONS OF VEGGIE FILLING AT ONE END OF THE LEAF. CAREFULLY ROLL THE LEAF TIGHTLY AND SECURE THE ENDS BY PUSHING THEM INTO THE ROLL.
9. PLACE ALL THE ROLLS IN A SAUCEPAN.
10. POUR IN THE WATER, ADD THE THYME AND BAY LEAF AND A PINCH OF SALT AND COOK THE CABBAGE ROLLS FOR 1 HOUR OR EVEN MORE AT LOW HEAT.
11. SERVE THE ROLLS WARM.

Couscous Stuffed Tomatoes

THIS DISH IS FRESH AND DELICIOUS, PERFECT FOR A LIGHT LUNCH OR DINNER. IT CAN EVEN BE SERVED AT PARTIES AS APPETIZERS. IT ALL DEPENDS ON HOW RICH THE STUFFING IS AND CONSIDERING THAT IT'S COUSCOUS THAT WE'RE TALKING ABOUT I HAVE TO SAY THAT IT CAN BE AS RICH AS YOU WANT – JUST ADD THE INGREDIENTS YOU FANCY THE MOST.

TIME: 40 MINUTES
SERVES: 10

INGREDIENTS:
1 ½ CUPS COUSCOUS
4 CUPS HOT VEGETABLE STOCK

1 CUP CANNED CHICKPEAS, DRAINED AND CHOPPED
1 CUP CHOPPED PARSLEY
1 CUP CHOPPED CILANTRO
¼ CUP CHOPPED MINT
1 LEMON, JUICED
SALT, PEPPER TO TASTE
½ CUP SLICED ALMONDS
8-10 RIPE TOMATOES

DIRECTIONS:
1. CUT THE TOP OF EACH TOMATO AND SCOOP OUT THE FLESH. SET THE TOMATOES ASIDE.
2. IN A LARGE BOWL, MIX THE COUSCOUS WITH THE HOT STOCK AND LET IT SOAK FOR 20 MINUTES.
3. FLUFF IT UP WITH A FORK AND STIR IN THE REST OF THE INGREDIENTS, EXCEPT THE ALMONDS.
4. ADJUST THE TASTE WITH SALT AND PEPPER THEN SPOON THE COUSCOUS INTO EACH TOMATO.
5. ARRANGE THE TOMATOES ON A PLATTER AND TOP EACH OF THEM WITH SLICED ALMONDS.
6. SERVE THE TOMATOES FRESH.

Basmati Rice with Potato Crust

TIME: 1 ¼ HOURS
SERVES: 6-8

INGREDIENTS:
1 CUP BASMATI RICE
4 CUPS VEGETABLE STOCK
4 TABLESPOONS OLIVE OIL
SALT, PEPPER TO TASTE
1 TEASPOON GARLIC POWDER
3 POTATOES, FINELY SLICED

DIRECTIONS:
1. COMBINE THE RICE WITH 3 CUPS STOCK, OLIVE OIL, SALT AND PEPPER IN A SAUCEPAN AND COOK UNTIL THE LIQUID IS ABSORBED.
2. REMOVE FROM HEAT AND SET ASIDE, STIRRING IN THE REMAINING STOCK.
3. ARRANGE THE POTATOES AT THE BOTTOM OF A PAN THAT CAN GO IN THE OVEN. SPRINKLE THEM WITH GARLIC POWDER THEN SPOON THE RICE OVER THE POTATOES.
4. BAKE IN THE PREHEATED OVEN AT 350F FOR 30 MINUTES.
5. WHEN DONE, REMOVE FROM THE OVEN AND TURN THE RICE UPSIDE DOWN ON A SERVING PLATTER.
6. SERVE THE RICE WARM.

Jeweled Rice

WHAT'S SPECIAL ABOUT THIS RICE IS HOW COLORFUL IT IS AND HOW FLAVORFUL. HAVING SO MANY VEGGIES IN ITS COMPOSITION MAKES IT AN EXCELLENT CHOICE FOR A HEALTHY LUNCH OR DINNER.

TIME: 1 HOUR
SERVES: 4-6

INGREDIENTS:
2 CUPS BASMATI RICE
6 CUPS WATER
1 TEASPOON SALT
¼ CUP OLIVE OIL
1 TEASPOON DEHYDRATED ONION
1 PINCH SAFFRON
1 ORANGE PEEL
1 CUP GREEN PEAS
1 CARROT, DICED
BLACK PEPPER TO TASTE

DIRECTIONS:
1. COMBINE THE RICE WITH THE WATER, SALT AND OLIVE OIL IN A SAUCEPAN AND COOK FOR 30 MINUTES ON LOW HEAT.
2. STIR IN THE REST OF THE INGREDIENTS AND COOK 15-20 MORE MINUTES.
3. SEASON WITH BLACK PEPPER AND SERVE THE RICE WARM.

Stuffed Eggplants

TIME: 1 ¼ HOURS
SERVES: 4

INGREDIENTS:
2 TABLESPOONS OLIVE OIL
1 SHALLOT, CHOPPED
1 GARLIC CLOVE, CHOPPED
1 RIPE TOMATO, DICED
1 CUP COOKED BASMATI RICE
1 CUP CHOPPED PARSLEY
1 TEASPOON DRIED MINT
SALT, PEPPER TO TASTE
2 EGGPLANTS

DIRECTIONS:
1. CUT THE EGGPLANTS IN HALF LENGTHWISE AND SCOOP OUT PART OF THE FLESH. CHOP IT FINELY.
2. HEAT THE OIL IN A SKILLET AND STIR IN THE SHALLOT, GARLIC AND EGGPLANT. SAUTÉ FOR 10 MINUTES, STIRRING OFTEN THEN ADD THE TOMATO, RICE, MINT AND PARSLEY.
3. SEASON WITH SALT AND PEPPER THEN REMOVE FROM HEAT AND SPOON THE MIXTURE BACK INTO THE EGGPLANT SKINS.
4. PLACE THEM ALL ON A BAKING TRAY LINED WITH PARCHMENT PAPER AND BAKE IN THE PREHEATED OVEN AT 350F FOR 40 MINUTES OR UNTIL SOFT.
5. REMOVE FROM THE OVEN AND SERVE THEM RIGHT AWAY.

Desserts
Persian Melon Popsicles

YOU WOULD NEVER THINK ABOUT COMBINING MELON THE WAY THIS RECIPE DOES. BUT ONCE YOU TASTE, YOU GET HOOKED, THAT GOOD AND FRESH IT TASTES. IT IS A GREAT RECIPE FOR SUMMER WHEN MELON IS AT ITS PEAKS.

TIME: 4 HOURS
SERVES: 6-8

INGREDIENTS:
1 MELON, PEELED AND CUBED
2 TABLESPOONS CHOPPED TARRAGON
4 TABLESPOONS AGAVE SYRUP

DIRECTIONS:
1. COMBINE ALL THE INGREDIENTS IN A BLENDER AND PROCESS UNTIL WELL BLENDED.
2. POUR THE MIXTURE IN POPSICLE MOLDS AND FREEZE AT LEAST 3 HOURS.
3. TO REMOVE THE POPSICLES FROM THEIR MOLDS, SINK THEM IN HOT WATER FOR 4-5 SECONDS.
4. SERVE THEM RIGHT AWAY.

Spiced Rice Pudding

TIME: 1 HOUR
SERVES: 4-6

INGREDIENTS:
1 CUP BASMATI RICE
3 CUPS ALMOND OR COCONUT MILK
2 CARDAMOM PODS, CRUSHED
½ CINNAMON STICK
¼ CUP AGAVE SYRUP
1 PINCH SALT
½ CUP SLICED ALMONDS FOR SERVING

DIRECTIONS:
1. RINSE THE RICE WELL AND MIX IT WITH THE MILK IN A HEAVY SAUCEPAN.
2. STIR IN THE AGAVE SYRUP, CARDAMOM AND CINNAMON THEN COOK THE RICE ON LOW HEAT FOR 30-40 MINUTES UNTIL MOST OF THE LIQUID HAS BEEN ABSORBED.
3. ADD A PINCH OF SALT TO BALANCE OUT THE TASTE THEN POUR THE PUDDING IN SERVING BOWLS.
4. TOP WITH SLICED ALMONDS JUST BEFORE SERVING.

Persian Chickpea Flour Cookies

ALTHOUGH THE INGREDIENT LIST IS SLIGHTLY UNUSUAL, THE COOKIES TURN OUT UNEXPECTEDLY TASTY. THEY ARE CRUMBLY AND FLAVORFUL AND THE TASTE IS RATHER EARTHY. THE NUTRITIONAL CONTENT IS HIGH AND THESE COOKIES CAN BECOME GREAT AFTERNOON SNACKS TO CALM YOUR SWEET CRAVINGS.

TIME: 45 MINUTES
YIELDS: 2 DOZEN

INGREDIENTS:
1 CUP COCONUT OIL, SOLID
½ CUP AGAVE SYRUP
2 TABLESPOONS GROUND FLAX SEEDS
1 TEASPOON GROUND CARDAMOM
½ TEASPOON CINNAMON POWDER
2 CUPS CHICKPEA FLOUR
1 PINCH SALT
½ TEASPOON BAKING SODA

DIRECTIONS:
1. COMBINE THE COCONUT OIL WITH THE AGAVE SYRUP IN A BOWL AND MIX WELL.
2. STIR IN THE REST OF THE INGREDIENTS AND MIX VERY WELL.
3. DROP SPOONFULS OF BATTER ON A BAKING TRAY LINED WITH PARCHMENT PAPER AND BAKE THE COOKIES IN THE PREHEATED OVEN AT 350F FOR 20-25 MINUTES.
4. REMOVE FROM THE OVEN WHEN THE EDGES TURN GOLDEN BROWN AND LET THEM COOL DOWN BEFORE SERVING OR STORING IN

AN AIRTIGHT CONTAINER FOR UP TO 1 WEEK.

Persian Halva

HALVA IS AN ORIENTAL DESSERT MADE NOT ONLY IN PERSIA, BUT ALSO IN ISRAEL, IRAQ, IRAN AND TURKEY FOR DECADES NOW. IT'S A SWEET AND FRAGRANT DESSERT THAT TASTES BETTER SERVED CHILLED.

TIME: 1 HOUR
SERVES: 4-6

INGREDIENTS:
1 ½ CUPS ALL-PURPOSE FLOUR
1 CUP AGAVE SYRUP
1 CUP WATER
1 CUP VEGETABLE OIL
1 TEASPOON SAFFRON
1 TEASPOON ROSE WATER

½ CUP PISTACHIO, SHELLED AND CHOPPED
½ CUP SLICED ALMONDS
¼ CUP RAISINS
1 PINCH SALT

DIRECTIONS:
1. HEAT THE OIL IN A SAUCEPAN AND STIR IN THE FLOUR AND SALT. SAUTÉ, STIRRING OFTEN, UNTIL IT BEGINS TO TURN GOLDEN.
2. IN A DIFFERENT SAUCEPAN, COMBINE THE SYRUP WITH 1 CUP WATER AND BRING TO A BOIL. COOK FOR 5 MINUTES THEN ADD THE SAFFRON AND ROSE WATER.
3. POUR THE HOT SYRUP OVER THE FLOUR AND COOK UNTIL IT BEGINS TO THICKEN.
4. STIR IN THE PISTACHIO, RAISINS AND ALMONDS.
5. SPOON THE MIXTURE IN SMALL SERVING BOWLS OR MOLDS AND LET THEM COOL DOWN BEFORE SERVING.
6. IT CAN BE SERVED EITHER SIMPLE OR WITH FRESH FRUITS.

Spiced Carrot Halva

SIMILAR TO THE WHEAT HALVA IN TERMS OF COOKING TECHNIQUE, THIS CARROT HALVA HAS A SPICED, INTENSE TASTE AND IT IS SOMEHOW LIGHTER, THE TASTE IS FRESHER AND THE HALVA ALSO HAS A BEAUTIFUL ORANGE COLOR WHICH MAKES IT FAR MORE APPEALING. I GUESS YOU HAVE TO TRY BOTH RECIPES THEN DECIDE WHICH ONE YOU LIKE MORE.

TIME: 1 HOUR
SERVES: 4-6

INGREDIENTS:
4 CUPS GRATED CARROTS
3 CUPS ALMOND MILK
¾ CUP AGAVE SYRUP
½ CUP VEGETABLE OIL
½ CUP WALNUTS, CHOPPED
½ TEASPOON CARDAMOM POWDER
½ TEASPOON CINNAMON POWDER
1 PINCH NUTMEG

DIRECTIONS:
1. COMBINE THE MILK WITH THE AGAVE SYRUP AND BRING TO A BOIL.
2. HEAT THE OIL IN A HEAVY SAUCEPAN AND STIR IN THE CARROTS. SAUTÉ FOR 10 MINUTES THEN POUR IN THE SYRUP AND KEEP COOKING FOR 20-30 MINUTES UNTIL THE MIXTURE BEGINS TO THICKEN.
3. REMOVE FROM HEAT AND STIR IN THE WALNUTS AND SPICES.
4. SPOON THE HALVA IN INDIVIDUAL SERVING BOWLS AND LET IT COOL DOWN COMPLETELY

BEFORE SERVING.

Cinnamon Date Cake

TIME: 1 HOUR
SERVES: 6-8

INGREDIENTS:
3 CUPS PITTED DATES
1 CUP WALNUTS, CHOPPED
1 CUP COCONUT OIL, MELTED
1 ½ CUPS ALL-PURPOSE FLOUR
½ CUP AGAVE SYRUP
1 TEASPOON CINNAMON POWDER
½ TEASPOON GROUND CARDAMOM
1 PINCH SALT
1 TEASPOON BAKING SODA
1 CUP COCONUT, SHREDDED
1 CUP PISTACHIO, CHOPPED

DIRECTIONS:
1. COMBINE THE DATES WITH THE WALNUTS, COCONUT OIL AND AGAVE SYRUP IN A FOOD PROCESSOR OR BLENDER AND PULSE UNTIL SMOOTH.
2. STIR IN THE FLOUR, SPICES, SALT AND BAKING POWDER THEN FOLD IN THE SHREDDED COCONUT AND PISTACHIO.
3. SPOON THE BATTER IN A ROUND CAKE PAN LINED WITH PARCHMENT PAPER.
4. BAKE THE CAKE IN THE PREHEATED OVEN AT 350F FOR 30-40 MINUTES.
5. TO CHECK IF THE CAKE IS DONE, INSERT A TOOTHPICK IN THE CENTER OF THE CAKE. IF IT COMES OUT CLEAN, THE CAKE IS DONE BUT IF IT STILL HAS TRACES OF BATTER, BAKE THE CAKE A FEW MORE MINUTES THEN CHECK AGAIN.

6. WHEN DONE, REMOVE FROM THE OVEN AND LET IT COOL DOWN BEFORE SLICING AND SERVING.

Wild Rice Apricot Pudding

TIME: 50 MINUTES
SERVES: 4-6

INGREDIENTS:
1 CUP WILD RICE
3 CUPS ALMOND MILK
2 TABLESPOONS CORNSTARCH
½ CUP AGAVE SYRUP
½ TEASPOON VANILLA EXTRACT
½ CUP SLICED ALMONDS FOR SERVING
½ CUP APRICOT JAM

DIRECTIONS:
1. COMBINE THE RICE WITH THE MILK IN A HEAVY SAUCEPAN AND BRING TO A BOIL. LOWER THE HEAT AND COOK THE RICE FOR 20-30 MINUTES UNTIL MOST OF THE LIQUID HAS BEEN ABSORBED.
2. STIR IN THE CORNSTARCH AND AGAVE SYRUP AND COOK A FEW MORE MINUTES UNTIL IT THICKENS.
3. REMOVE FROM HEAT AND STIR IN THE VANILLA. SPOON THE PUDDING IN INDIVIDUAL SERVING BOWLS AND LET THEM COOL DOWN BEFORE SERVING.
4. TOP WITH APRICOT JAM AND SLICED ALMONDS JUST BEFORE SERVING IT.

Melon and Cherry Compote

COMPOTE IS AMAZING DURING SUMMER, ESPECIALLY SERVED CHILLED. IT IS A VERSATILE RECIPE AND YOU CAN APPLY THIS COOKING TECHNIQUE TO MANY OTHER FRUITS, FROM PEACHES TO APRICOTS, SOUR CHERRIES OR GRAPES.

TIME: 30 MINUTES
SERVES: 2-4

INGREDIENTS:
2 CUPS MELON CUBES
2 CUPS CHERRIES
1 CUP WATER
1 CUP ORANGE JUICE
2 TABLESPOONS AGAVE SYRUP
½ CINNAMON STICK
1 STAR ANISE
1 LEMON SLICE

DIRECTIONS:
1. COMBINE THE MELON WITH THE CHERRIES, WATER AND ORANGE JUICE IN A SAUCEPAN.
2. STIR IN THE AGAVE SYRUP, CINNAMON STICK, LEMON SLICE AND STAR ANISE AND BRING TO BOIL.
3. COOK THE COMPOTE FOR 20 MINUTES ON LOW HEAT, MAKING SURE THE FRUITS ARE TENDER BUT NOT MUSHY.
4. REMOVE FROM HEAT AND DISCARD THE CINNAMON STICK, LEMON SLICE AND STAR ANISE.
5. LET IT COOL DOWN THEN SERVE CHILLED.

Persian Sweet Rice

TIME: 1 HOUR
SERVES: 4-6

INGREDIENTS:
1 ½ CUPS BASMATI RICE, RINSED
¼ CUP COCONUT OIL
½ CUP AGAVE SYRUP
2 CUPS GRATED CARROTS
½ CUP SLICED ALMONDS
½ CUP CHOPPED DATES
½ CUP CHOPPED DRIED FIGS
¼ CUP PUMPKIN SEEDS
1 TEASPOON GROUND CARDAMOM
½ TEASPOON CINNAMON POWDER
1 TEASPOON TURMERIC

DIRECTIONS:
1. STEAM THE RICE UNTIL SOFT AND FLUFFED UP. REMOVE FROM HEAT AND FLUFF IT UP WITH A FORK THEN SET ASIDE.
2. HEAT THE OIL IN A SKILLET AND STIR IN THE CARROTS. SAUTÉ FOR 10 MINUTES THEN ADD THE REST OF THE INGREDIENTS.
3. COOK FOR 10 MORE MINUTES THEN STIR IN THE RICE.
4. SAUTÉ FOR 15 MINUTES, STIRRING OFTEN THEN REMOVE FROM HEAT AND SERVE THE RICE WARM OR CHILLED.

Ranginak – Date and Walnut Squares

TIME: 1 HOUR
SERVES: 4-6

INGREDIENTS:
2 CUPS ALL-PURPOSE FLOUR
2 CUPS PITTED DATES
½ CUP AGAVE SYRUP
1 CUP WALNUTS, GROUND
1 TEASPOON CINNAMON POWDER
½ TEASPOON CARDAMOM POWDER
1 CUP VEGETABLE OIL
1 PINCH SALT

DIRECTIONS:
1. HEAT THE OIL IN A HEAVY SAUCEPAN AND STIR IN THE FLOUR. COOK FOR 15-20 MINUTES, STIRRING OFTEN, UNTIL THE FLOUR TURNS GOLDEN BROWN. STIR IN THE AGAVE SYRUP AND WALNUTS, AS WELL AS THE SPICES AND A PINCH OF SALT.
2. REMOVE FROM HEAT AND SPREAD HALF OF THE MIXTURE IN A SQUARE PAN.
3. TOP WITH PITTED DATES THEN COVER WITH THE REMAINING FLOUR MIXTURE.
4. REFRIGERATE 1 HOUR THEN CUT IN SMALL SQUARES AND SERVE.

Conclusion

THE PERSIAN CUISINE IS AN EXPLOSION OF COLOR AND FLAVOR, A CUISINE THAT IMPRESSES WITH EVERY ASPECT, FROM BALANCED SPICES TO BOLD FLAVORS AND UNUSUAL COMBINATIONS. BUT APART FROM THIS, IT IS A CUISINE BASED ON FRESH FRUITS AND VEGGIES MORE THAN ON ANYTHING ELSE AND THAT MAKES THE TRANSITION FROM A COMMON DIET TO A VEGAN ONE MUCH EASIER. SALADS, SOUPS, STEWS OR STUFFED VEGGIES ARE ALL EASY TO COOK AND OFFER AMAZING EATING EXPERIENCES FOR THE ENTIRE FAMILY.

ALL YOU HAVE TO DO IS PUT THAT APRON ON AND GET ADVENTUROUS IN THE KITCHEN! YOU HAVE NO IDEA HOW MUCH SATISFACTION COOKING SOMETHING FROM SCRATCH OFFERS YOU, ESPECIALLY WHEN WE ARE TALKING ABOUT SUCH FRAGRANT AND SPECIAL DISHES.

www.ingramcontent.com/pod-product-compliance
Lightning Source LLC
LaVergne TN
LVHW020419070526
838199LV00055B/3663